ROALD DAHL

A Real-Life Reader Biography

Ann Graham Gaines

Mitchell Lane Publishers, Inc.
P.O. Box 619
Bear, Delaware 19701

Mitchell Lane
PUBLISHERS

First Printing

Real-Life Reader Biographies

Paula Abdul	Mary Joe Fernandez	Ricky Martin	Arnold Schwarzenegger
Christina Aguilera	Andres Galarraga	Mark McGwire	Selena
Marc Anthony	Sarah Michelle Gellar	Alyssa Milano	Dr. Seuss
Drew Barrymore	Jeff Gordon	Mandy Moore	Shakira
Brandy	Mia Hamm	Chuck Norris	Alicia Silverstone
Garth Brooks	Melissa Joan Hart	Tommy Nuñez	Jessica Simpson
Kobe Bryant	Salma Hayek	Rosie O'Donnell	Sinbad
Sandra Bullock	Jennifer Love Hewitt	Rafael Palmeiro	Jimmy Smits
Mariah Carey	Hollywood Hogan	Gary Paulsen	Sammy Sosa
Cesar Chavez	Katie Holmes	Freddie Prinze, Jr.	Britney Spears
Christopher Paul Curtis	Enrique Iglesias	Julia Roberts	Sheryl Swoopes
Roald Dahl	Derek Jeter	Robert Rodriguez	Shania Twain
Oscar De La Hoya	Steve Jobs	J.K. Rowling	Liv Tyler
Trent Dimas	Michelle Kwan	Keri Russell	Robin Williams
Celine Dion	Bruce Lee	Winona Ryder	Vanessa Williams
Sheila E.	Jennifer Lopez	Cristina Saralegui	Tiger Woods
Gloria Estefan	Cheech Marin		

Library of Congress Cataloging-in-Publication Data
Gaines, Ann.
    Roald Dahl/Ann Graham Gaines.
       p. cm. — (A real-life reader biography)
    Includes bibliographical references and index.
    ISBN 1-58415-075-0
    1. Dahl, Roald—Juvenile literature. 2 Authors, English—20th century—Biography—Juvenile literature. 3. Children's stories—Authorship—Juvenile literature. [1. Dahl, Roald. 2. Authors, English.] I Title. II Series.
PR6054.A35 Z67 2001
823'914—dc21
   [B]
                                                   00-067807

ABOUT THE AUTHOR: Ann Gaines holds graduate degrees in American Civilization and Library and Information Science from the University of Texas at Austin. She has been a freelance writer for 18 years, specializing in nonfiction for children. She lives near Gonzales, Texas with her husband and their four children.

PHOTO CREDITS: cover: Archive Photos; p. 4 Archive Photos; p. 17 Corbis; pp. 26, 27, 28 AP.

ACKNOWLEDGMENTS: The following story has been thoroughly researched, and to the best of our knowledge, represents a true story. While every possible effort has been made to ensure accuracy, the publisher will not assume liability for damages caused by inaccuracies in the data, and makes no warranty on the accuracy of the information contained herein.

Table of Contents

Chapter 1
Whipple-Scrumptious Fudgemallow Delight

Roald (pronounced ROO-aal) Dahl, author of such great children's books as *James and the Giant Peach* and *Charlie and the Chocolate Factory,* had the most amazing ideas. He filled his stories with huge floating fruits, big friendly giants, talking turtles, and incredible candy. Many of his ideas came from his vivid imagination. But others were inspired by his own experiences.

One example is the whipple-scrumptious fudgemallow delight, a

Charlie and the Chocolate Factory is one of Roald Dahl's famous books.

mouth-watering candy Willy Wonka and the Oompah-Loompahs make in *Charlie and the Chocolate Factory*. When Charlie has the good fortune to be one of six children to win a tour of Mr. Wonka's candy factory, his favorite part of the whole day is seeing the testing room. There Wonka slaves over new inventions, trying to create the world's most perfect candy.

Of course there is nothing quite like Willy Wonka's chocolate factory in real life. Yet it was something that happened in Roald Dahl's life that gave him the idea for the testing room.

As a child, he actually was a chocolate tester. His mother had sent him off to boarding school. In many ways, it was a terrible time for him. He was homesick. His teachers punished pupils for even slight violations of their very strict rules by beating them with canes.

But he had some happy memories from that time, too. One was of the days when the chocolate boxes arrived. Every

The story of Charlie came from Roald's real life when he was a chocolate tester for Cadbury.

so often, the Cadbury company sent every boy at his school a box containing twelve chocolate bars. They came in many different shapes and fillings.

One would be a "control," a popular candy bar everybody already loved. But the other eleven would be brand-new experiments. Along with the chocolate bars came forms, on which the boys rated each bar from 1 to 10 and made comments. Those they liked soon went into production.

In later life, Roald Dahl said this was a brilliant move on the part of the Cadbury Company. After all, who knows more about candy than children? He and his fellow students were very glad to offer their opinions.

The chocolate testing inspired his fondest daydreams, he went on. When he wanted to escape from everyday life, he imagined the laboratory where all these delicacies were thought up. First he pictured men and women in white coats moving between bubbling pots of chocolate, fudge, raspberry syrup,

When Roald was in boarding school, he imagined a laboratory where all these candies were made.

It would be years later that Roald would invent *Charlie and the Chocolate Factory.*

vanilla cream, and other yummy flavors. Then he pictured himself as the greatest inventor of them all. Years later, when he was trying to think about for an idea for a new book for children, he remembered those daydreams. They were the inspiration, of course, for *Charlie and the Chocolate Factory.*

Chapter 2

Growing Up

Roald Dahl was born on September 13, 1916, in Llandaff, South Wales. Wales is one of four countries that make up Great Britain. The other countries are England, Northern Ireland, and Scotland. Wales is located on the west coast of Great Britain. Most of the people of Wales live in the coal-mining regions in southern Wales. His father, Harald Dahl, had been born in Norway. As a young man, Harald ran away from home. Eventually, he and a partner began selling everything that large ships needed. At that time, most ships used coal for power, so Harald settled in

Roald Dahl was born in Great Britain.

Cardiff, the capital of Wales. It was a big port near huge coal mines.

By this time, Harald Dahl had married a young woman named Marie. He had become a wealthy man so the couple bought an elegant house in a village named Llandaff, close to Cardiff. Their first child, a daughter, was born there. Soon Marie became pregnant with a son. Sadly, she died during his childbirth. Harald grieved terribly over her death. Nevertheless, he soon decided to find a new wife to help raise his two tiny children.

Thus in the summer of 1911, he went home to Norway to find his new bride. There he met Sofia Magdalene Hesselberg. Within a week, Harald had proposed to Sofie, as she was nicknamed.

Harald took his bride back to Wales. She had an easy time settling into the house in Llandaff and treated his children as if they were her own. This marriage may have started out as one of convenience. Yet it turned out very well.

Harald and Sofia came to love each other deeply. They had four children of their own. The first two were girls. Then came Roald and, finally, another daughter. This brought the total number of children in the household to six.

The family was very happy. Their parents doted on the children and they all enjoyed spending time together. Inside, they read, played games, and watched Harald paint. The family also spent a great deal of time outside, taking long walks and exploring the beach.

Unfortunately, in 1920, when Roald was 3, tragedy struck the family again. His older sister, Astri, suddenly died from appendicitis. She was seven. She had been Harald's favorite child and he was grief-stricken. A month later, he became ill himself from pneumonia and died soon afterward.

Harald Dahl had always wanted his children to be educated in England. "He maintained that there was some kind of magic about English schooling and that the education it provided had caused

But there was tragedy, as well. Roald's sister and father died very suddenly in 1920.

the inhabitants of a small island to become a great nation and to produce the world's greatest literature," Roald once wrote of his father.

Sofie wanted to honor Harald's wish to have his children go to school in England so she decided to stay in Wales rather than move the family to Norway, even though it was hard for her to raise five children by herself. She would carry out his plan.

But she would make sure the children knew Norway, too. They spent every single summer there, in a hotel on what they called "Magic Island." There the family beachcombed, swam, boated, and explored the many nearby islands.

They returned each fall in time for school. Roald began kindergarten in Llandaff at the age of six. At seven, he moved to a preparatory school called Llandaff Cathedral School. There he made many friends. They loved to go to the sweet-shop together, even though it was run by a horrible woman named Mrs. Pratchett. Dahl remembered that

His father had always wanted his children to be educated in England.

she only spoke to them to say, "I'm watchin' you so keep yer thievin' fingers off them chocolates" and such. Once he got in terrible trouble when he put a dead mouse in one of her big jars.

In 1925, his mother sent him away to St. Peters Boarding School. To get to the school in Weston-Super-Mare, on the coast of England, he rode a paddlewheel steamer. It wasn't a happy time in his life.

Looking back, he would remember, "Those were days of horrors, of fierce discipline, of not talking in the dormitories, no running in the corridors, no untidiness of any sort, no this or that or the other, just rules, rules and still more rules that had to be obeyed. And the fear of the dreaded cane hung over us."

Boys would be called to the office of the headmaster when they didn't obey those rules and beaten. Dahl described the pain of the cane "as though someone had laid a white-hot poker across your backside and pressed hard."

In 1925, Roald was sent to a boarding school in England. The school was very strict and Roald did not have many happy memories of this time.

At the age of 13, he enrolled in a new school called Repton, one of the best private schools in all of England. The beatings from teachers and older students were even worse than before. But he stayed there until he graduated.

At that time, Dahl had no idea that he would ever become a writer. In fact, his English Composition teachers said things like, "He seems incapable of marshalling his thoughts on paper," and "Consistently idle. Ideas limited."

Chapter 3
Off to Africa

Most graduates of Repton went on to a university. Roald Dahl's mother would have liked for him to do the same thing. But what he wanted was to work overseas in an exotic place like Asia or Africa.

"So during my last term I applied for a job only to those companies that would be sure to send me abroad," he said. One of those companies was Shell Oil and he beat out many other applicants to land a position with them.

Shell gave him two years of training. First he went to a refinery where he

When Roald graduated from high school, he wanted to go overseas for adventure.

learned all about different kinds of fuel. Then he reported to the company's headquarters in London, to learn about being a salesman, keeping accounts, and things like that.

In 1937, Shell sent him to East Africa. In those days, few airplanes carried passengers between Europe and Africa. Instead he boarded a ship for a voyage of two and a half weeks to Mombasa, in Kenya. From there he took a little coastal vessel to Dar-es-Salaam, in the country then called Tanganyika but today called Tanzania.

He was one of three Shell Oil employees who lived in a company house. From Dar-es-Salaam he would drive out in the company station wagon. On trips that could last for a month or more, he visited sisal (a plant whose leaves were used to make fiber) and cotton plantations, gold and diamond mines, and many other businesses. He supplied them all with fuel they needed for their vehicles and lubricating oil for their heavy machinery. Later he would

He got a job with Shell Oil Company so he could travel.

say that the job did not require much in terms of intelligence or imagination, "but by gum you needed to be fit and tough." One wonderful part of the job was the chance it offered him to see wildlife while he was driving: giraffes, elephants, hippos, zebras, antelope, and every once in awhile, even lions.

Roald loved adventure and travel, but when he was in school, his teachers did not see any potential in his writing.

While in Africa, he kept up with the news from Europe by reading newspapers and listening to the radio. By the summer of 1939, the news was grim. War loomed. Adolf Hitler had become dictator in Germany and formed an alliance with Italy which Japan soon joined. The Axis countries, as they were called, planned to invade other countries. To fight back, France, Great Britain, the Soviet Union, and later the United

States formed their own alliance. They were known as the Allies.

When it was clear that war was about to break out, the British government ordered its young men living in East Africa to prepare to fight. Dahl was given a platoon of native men to command. He had no experience fighting, but his men did and they were armed with rifles and a machine gun.

But his peaceful life was disrupted by the war brewing in Europe.

His platoon was given orders to guard the road that led from British East Africa into Portuguese East Africa. They were to prevent Germans from escaping there. The British government did not want Germans to be able to go home and join the German military. On the day when Great Britain declared war on Germany, hundreds of Germans did try to escape down the road. But Dahl and his men captured them without incident.

Chapter 4
War!

After the Germans had been taken to a prisoner of war camp, Dahl drove hundreds of miles north to Nairobi, Kenya. There he joined the British Royal Air Force and was trained to fly fighter planes. These planes carried just one man, the pilot. After only seven hours and forty minutes of flying time in a training plane, Dahl went up in the air by himself. He spent the next several weeks perfecting his flying skills. He learned to loop the loop, fly upside down, and pull out of a downward spin. Then he was sent to his first station in

Dahl joined the British Royal Air Force and was trained to fly fighter planes.

Egypt, where he learned to fly older planes called Gladiators. They were biplanes, which means they had two wings, and were armed with two machine guns.

Soon he was sent to join a new squadron. But when he landed at a British base to refuel, he was given wrong information concerning the squadron's location. Following those instructions, he flew into a no-man's-land between the British and Italian armies. He flew all around, looking for the squadron, but it was nowhere to be found.

He searched until his plane was about to run out of fuel and night was about to fall. He realized he would have to make a forced landing. From the air, he could see that the sand was littered with boulders and gulleys. But he had no choice. So he slowed his engine and landed. But on the ground, the plane kept moving. Rolling along at 75 miles an hour, it hit a boulder and came to a sudden stop.

He learned to fly planes called Gladiators.

Dahl's face hit the windshield, breaking his nose and knocking out several of his teeth. His eyes also suffered so terribly in the impact that he was temporarily blinded. Suddenly he heard one of his gas tanks explode. He knew the entire plane was about to blow up, so he undid his seat belts, took off his parachute, pushed himself up and out of the cockpit, and rolled out onto the sand. He dragged himself away from the plane just as fast as he could. His machine gun ammunition exploded in the heat. Finally he collapsed. He might have died, except for the fact that people could see the flames from his plane for miles around. In the night, three British soldiers rescued him. He went first to an underground first-aid post and then onto a hospital in Alexandria, Egypt. After six months of physical therapy, during which he slowly regained his sight, he was sent back out to the war in Greece and given a new, much more powerful airplane to fly, called a Hurricane.

One day his plane crashed and three British soldiers rescued him.

In Greece he flew more dangerous missions and shot down several German planes. But the Germans heavily outnumbered the Greek and British defenders, and quickly won the battle there. Dahl and the few pilots who had survived were sent to Palestine (modern-day Israel). But he often had blackouts in mid-air as a result of his earlier crash. Finally he had to stop fighting. So he became an air attache for the British government in Washington, D.C. This meant he helped to make Americans aware of what the British and American air forces were doing in the war.

Chapter 5
Becoming a Children's Writer

It was in Washington, D.C., that Roald Dahl would take his first step toward becoming a writer. One day a famous British author named C.S. Forester came to see Dahl in his office. Forester was the author of a long series of exciting adventure books featuring a naval officer named Horatio Hornblower. Dahl admired him very much.

Forester would have liked to fight in the war like Dahl, but he was too old. Instead he was writing newspaper stories and articles about brave British

One day a famous author named C.S. Forester came to see Roald.

soldiers, sailors, and pilots. The United States had just entered the war. Forester wanted to inspire Americans to support the war effort. In the hopes that Dahl would have stories to tell him, Forester invited the young man to lunch.

Forester started to take notes about Dahl's crash in the desert, but became distracted when their meal arrived. So Dahl volunteered to write it down later. That night, he got to work. Forester had asked him to provide plenty of detail. Dahl found it easy. "The story seemed to be telling itself, and the hand that held the pencil moved rapidly back and forth across each page," he said. The next day he sent it off.

Forester wrote back two weeks later. He said, "Dear RD, You were meant to give me notes, not a finished story. I'm bowled over. Your piece is marvelous." He finished by saying that he had sent it on as Dahl had written it to the *Saturday Evening Post* and he enclosed a check for $900 for the article. Sure enough, the piece appeared in the *Post* under Dahl's

His first story was published by *The Saturday Evening Post*.

name, but an editor had beefed it up. To make it even more exciting, he made it appear that Dahl had been shot down by the enemy.

Thus began Dahl's writing career. In the years that followed, he continued to write, inspired by his first check. At first he wrote mostly short stories for grown-ups. He wrote fiction about flying, mysteries, and humorous stories.

But later in 1942, he did write one story for children. It was called "The Gremlins" and it was about tiny men who lived on airplanes and sabotaged them, causing them to crash. Dahl's story appeared first in a magazine and was then bought by Walt Disney, who intended to use it as the basis for a movie. The movie was never finished, but Disney published Dahl's story as a book and it became immensely popular.

Dahl then went back to writing for grown-ups. He had many stories and books appear. In 1953, he married a famous actress named Patricia Neal. Altogether they would have five

Inspired by his first check, Roald continued to write.

children, including four daughters and a son. Their names were Olivia, Tessa, Theo, Ophelia, and Lucy. But in many ways, their marriage was a sad one.

In the summer of 1960, Dahl and the family were living in New York City. Theo was still a baby. One day a taxicab hit his baby carriage. He suffered massive head injuries and became brain-damaged, from which he would never recover. Then in 1962, Ophelia died at age 7 of measles.

Three years later, while pregnant, Patricia suffered three strokes on a single day. She had to remain under the care of doctors and nurses for years. Roald Dahl would be very involved in her care and she would recover partly due to his efforts. To this day, methods he invented to help her regain her ability to speak and move about are used in clinics and hospitals the world over.

Patricia Neal suffered a stroke and took years to recover. Here are Roald and three children: Ophelia, 11 months, Tessa, 8 and Theo, 5.

By 1968, Patricia Neal was well enough to star in another movie. She is seen here attending the New York premiere of The Subject Was Roses.

Even in the midst of all this, Dahl continued to work. In the early 1960s, he hosted a television series called *Way Out*. He continued to write for grown-ups, but having his own children had also inspired him to try to write for a younger audience. In 1961, his first children's novel appeared. It was *James and the Giant Peach* and was based on bedtime stories he had made up for his own children.

Chapter 6
Fame

James and the Giant Peach made Roald Dahl a famous children's author. Over the next 30 years, he wrote 25 more books for children. Beginning in the mid-1970s, an artist named Quentin Blake did most of the illustrations for his book. Their styles jived extremely well. Dahl continued to write for grown-ups as well. And he wrote screenplays. Two were for children's movies: first, *Chitty Chitty Bang Bang* and then *Willie Wonka and the Chocolate Factory*, based on his own book.

James and the Giant Peach made Roald a famous children's author.

But he received the most satisfaction from — and the most acclaim for — his children's books. Children would always love his wild, fantastic stories filled with plot twists and turns. One thing that they especially liked was that cruel adults who did bad things to children were eventually punished for their wickedness.

Roald Dahl loved the many letters and cards he received from children. He not only liked to go to meet young readers at schools and libraries, but he also donated a great deal of time and money to children's groups and charities.

Ironically, even though his books encouraged many, many children to read, they would receive mixed reviews from educators and librarians. Some grownups worried that he too often told stories in which adults were bad guys. They complained that he showed contempt for institutions like schools.

But Dahl paid little attention to them. He always wrote to please himself and his audience of children, rather than critics. And along the way, he would be rewarded with many prestigious literary awards, including England's Whitbread Prize and the Children's Book Award.

When Roald Dahl died on November 23, 1990, he was still in the middle of a project. His last book, *The Vicar of Nibbleswicke*, appeared only after his death. Today many of his children's books remain in great demand. They seem destined to become classics of children's literature.

Selected List of Children's Books

The BFG, with pictures by Quentin Blake (New York : Farrar, Straus, Giroux, 1982).
Boy: Tales of Childhood (New York: Farrar, Straus, Giroux, 1984).
Charlie and the Chocolate Factory (New York: Knopf, 1964).
Charlie and the Great Glass Elevator (New York: Knopf, 1972).
Danny, the Champion of the World (New York: Knopf, 1975).
The Enormous Crocodile (New York: Puffin Books, 1993).
Fantastic Mr. Fox (New York: Knopf, 1970).
George's Marvelous Medicine (New York: Knopf, 1982, c1981).
Giraffe and the Pelly and Me (New York: Knopf, 1985).
Going Solo (New York: Farrar, Straus, Giroux, 1986).
James and the Giant Peach (New York: Knopf, 1961).
Matilda (New York: Viking Kestrel, 1988).
The Twits (New York: Knopf, 1981, c1980).
The Vicar of Nibbleswicke (New York: Viking, 1992).
The Witches (New York: Farrar, Straus, Giroux, 1983).
Wonderful World of Henry Sugar, And Six More (New York: Knopf, 1977).

Chronology

- 1916, born on September 13, in Llandaff, South Wales.
- 1920, sister and then his father die very suddenly.
- 1922, starts kindergarten.
- 1925, sent away to boarding school.
- 1934, graduates from Repton School and goes to work for Shell Oil in London.
- 1937, goes to Africa to work for Shell Oil.
- 1939, joins the Royal Air Force to fight in World War II.
- 1942, publishes first piece of writing in *The Saturday Evening Post*. Later that year, sells his very first story for children, "The Gremlins," to Walt Disney.
- 1953, marries actress Patricia Neal
- 1961, publishes *James and the Giant Peach*, his first novel for children. Twenty-five more children's books would follow.
- 1983, divorces Patricia Neal and marries Felicity Ann Crosland.
- 1990, dies November 23, at age 74.

Index